NOËL COWARD

A Life in Quotes

NOËL COWARD

A Life in Quotes

——

COMPILED AND
INTRODUCED BY
BARRY DAY

★ ★
★

metro

First published in Great Britain in 1999
by Metro Books (an imprint of Metro Publishing Limited),
19 Gerrard Street, London W1V 7LA

Barry Day is hereby identified as the author of this work in accordance
with Section 77 of the Copyright, Designs and Patents Act 1988.

The publishers are grateful to Methuen for permission to reprint extracts
from Coward's plays, verse, lyrics and autobiography, and to Weidenfeld &
Nicolson for permission to reprint extracts from the *Diaries*.

Caricatures on pages 1, 76 and 89 by Clive Francis. Illustration on page 94
by Marc reproduced by kind permission.

The author and publishers have made every effort to ascertain and acknowledge the copyright-holders of material included in this book. Any errors or
omissions that have inadvertently occurred will be rectified in future editions,
provided that prior written notification is sent to the publishers.

British Library Cataloguing in Publication Data.
A CIP record of this book is available on request from the British Library.

ISBN 1 900512 84 X

10 9 8 7 6 5 4 3 2

Designed and typeset in Monotype Perpetua by Ken Wilson

Printed in Great Britain by CPD Group, Wales

How invaluable it would be... if just once, for a brief spell, I could see myself clearly from the outside, as others saw me. How helpful it would be, moving so continually across the public vision, to know what that vision really observed, to note objectively what it was in my personality that moved some people to like and applaud me and aroused in others such irritation and resentment. How salutary it would be to watch the whole performance through from the front of the house, to see to what extent the mannerisms were effective and note when and where they should be cut down.

Future Indefinite (1954)

CONTENTS

★

INTRODUCTION

—

The Word According to Coward

★

DID NOËL COWARD use the words – or did the words use him?

Certainly, you'd be hard put to name anyone in the twentieth century who employed the English language with the same precision, concision and consistency as he did. And his range was remarkable. In the dialogue of his plays, in verse, song lyrics, essays, stories, letters, autobiography, interviews – and perhaps most particularly in private conversation – words were his weapons, and 'wordsmith' both his occupation and his preoccupation.

An essentially private person for so public a persona, he consistently used the words to create an image behind which he could hide his more vulnerable emotions. So effective was this defence mechanism that Coward has rarely been given the credit for even possessing ordinary sensibilities – although he provided a clue to the contrary in one of his plays. In *Shadow Play* he has Gertrude Lawrence say: 'Small talk, a lot of small talk with other thoughts going on behind.' The small talk and the apparent frivolity are what we say when to say what we really *mean* would prove too painful.

American novelist Peter de Vries once skewered one of his own characters by saying that 'on the surface he was deep – but deep down he was shallow'. Precisely the opposite was true of Noël Coward but, ironically, it was largely the posthumous publication of his *Diaries* and a study of his private papers that provided the portrait with its present light and shade.

Coward was a curious man – in the strict sense of that word. He was fascinated by the people with whom he shared the planet, by the feelings they apparently had in common and the behaviour – particularly the patterns of speech – that differentiated them, so that the same words from different speakers could convey quite different meanings. And everything he saw and heard he recorded.

One speech in *Present Laughter* (1939) will serve as an example. The actor Garry Essendine is making stilted small talk with the aspiring young playwright Roland Maule:

GARRY: You've come all the way from Uckfield?

ROLAND: It isn't very far.

GARRY: Well, it sort of *sounds* far, doesn't it?

ROLAND (*defensively*): It's quite near Lewes.

GARRY: Then there's nothing to worry about, is there?

[*x*]

A sociological thesis couldn't define the two characters more precisely.

Coward is generally considered a man who lived in and for the moment. In fact, he never forgot a humble past and constantly recreated it in his depiction (often more nostalgically affectionate than realistic) of working-class life. He was also concerned – increasingly so as the years went by – with the purpose of life. Among the earliest musings he privately committed to youthful paper, he debates with himself the value of religion. In public, the instinctive barrier of words is erected.

Did he believe in God?, David Frost once asked him in a television interview. 'We've never been intimate – but maybe we do have a few things in common,' Noël replied, lighting the ever-present cigarette and disappearing behind a cloud of smoke.

In a later interview he was asked for the one valedictory word he felt would sum up the play that had been his life. He bought himself a little time by pondering aloud the risk of sounding 'corny' before settling on: 'LOVE... To know that you are among people whom you love and who love you. That has made all the successes wonderful – much more wonderful than they'd have been anyway. And I don't think there's anything more to be said after that.'

Seen in this light, Coward's use of words is significantly different from that of the two writers with whom he is most often compared. A Wilde epigram may have a greater surface shine, but drop it and all you are left with are fragments. Pick up one by Shaw and you may well cut yourself, for it lacks kindness. Coward is altogether more comfortable company because his is the language of the good conversationalist and the kind man; his *bons mots* deal with the stuff of all our lives, and perhaps what defines him most is that you feel you have thought these thoughts and might have expressed many of them yourself – if only the words had fallen in the right order.

In this collection I have naturally included many of the 'classic' Coward lines but I have also delved into the private papers and unpublished material for lines that – even out of context – show a mind in the making and the emergence of themes he would re-orchestrate and refine as the years went by. Where possible I have attributed the quotations to their specific context but inevitably – as with all the great wits – some have become part of the legend by word of mouth. Coward himself summed up the dilemma best when he declared: 'I'm naturally a witty man. I have been and doubtless I always shall be. In my time I've said some noteworthy and exceptionally memorable things. If the remarks with which I am credited – and never made – are really good, I acknowledge them. I generally work myself into the belief that I originally said them.'

I think you will find that *A Life in Quotes* reveals more than merely a unique wit – the precious commodity he always felt should be 'a glorious treat like caviar', not 'spread about like marmalade'. It depicts a man of depth, compassion and London pride. After the 'cocktails and laughter' there was infinitely more than 'just a talent to amuse'.

Barry Day

1999

'Why Must
the Show
Go On?'

★

TO COWARD, the theatre was virtually a religion, a 'temple of illusion', and he could not bear to see that temple desecrated by Philistines, either from within or from without. Typically, his punishment was ridicule.

Genuine lack of talent always appalled him, as did some of the theatre's more arcane traditions. After half a century of watching gallant 'troupers', young or old, dragging themselves through their 'Laugh, Clown, Laugh' routines to ensure that the show went on regardless, he decided he had finally had enough and, in a song in his Café de Paris cabaret act in the early 1950s, he posed the question no one was meant to ask:

> *Why must the show go on?*
> *It can't be all that indispensable,*
> *To me it really isn't sensible*
> *On the whole*
> *To play a leading role*
> *While fighting those tears you can't*
>   *control,*
> *Why kick up your legs*
> *When draining the dregs*
> *Of sorrow's bitter cup?*
> *Because you have read*
> *Some idiot has said*
> *'The Curtain must go up!'*
> 'Why Must the Show Go On?' (1954)

Not that his own career ran entirely smoothly:

I partnered a girl name Eileen Dennis,
and we were engaged by the Elysée
Restaurant (now the Café de Paris) to
appear during dinner and supper. A slow
waltz, a tango, and a rather untidy one-
step made up our programme. Later,
owing to popular demand (from Eileen
Dennis's mother), we introduced a
pierrot fantasia for which we changed
into cherry-coloured sateen and tulle
ruffs. No South African millionaires
threw diamond sunbursts at Eileen's
feet. We were neither of us ever invited
to appear naked out of pies at private
supper parties, in fact the whole
engagement from the point of view of
worldly experience was decidedly
disappointing.

Present Indicative (1937)

His début came at a ridiculously early age and he would
look back on his younger self with awed objectivity:

I was a brazen, odious little prodigy,
overpleased with myself and precocious
to a degree.

MR. NOËL COWARD MAKING MENTAL NOTES
FOR THE FIRST PART OF "CAVALCADE."

Reflecting on an early performance:

> I am certain that, could my adult self
> have been present… he would have
> crept out, at the first coy gurgle, and
> been mercifully sick outside.

Present Indicative (1937)

On playing Slightly:

> Forty years ago he was Slightly in *Peter Pan*, and you might say that he has been wholly in *Peter Pan* ever since.
> Kenneth Tynan

★　★　★

> It really is unbelievably difficult to act like a moron when one isn't a moron.
> To a child actor colleague, Míchaél Mac Liammóir

★　★　★

> PERRY: I love *Peter Pan*.
> ZELDA: That's because you've got a mother-fixation. All sensitive lads with mother-fixations worship *Peter Pan*.
> *Waiting in the Wings* (1960)

As a child actor himself under the eagle eye of a 'stage mother' he had plenty of opportunity to study the phenomenon at close quarters as audition succeeded audition:

> *Don't put your daughter on the stage,*
> *Mrs Worthington,*
> *Don't put your daughter on the stage,*
> *The profession is overcrowded*

[6]

And the struggle's pretty tough
And admitting the fact
She's burning to act
That isn't quite enough.
'Mrs Worthington'
(1936)

It was rarely a pretty sight and the song was his attempt to provide a corrective:

It is a genuine *cri de coeur*... Unhappily, its effectiveness, from the point of view of propaganda, has been negligible. I had hoped, by writing it, to discourage misguided maternal ambition, to deter those dreadful eager mothers from making beasts of themselves, boring the hell out of me and wasting their own and my time, but I have not succeeded ... ninety-nine out of a hundred of the letters they write to me refer to it with roguish indulgence, obviously secure in the conviction that it could not in any circumstance apply to them. This is saddening, of course, but realising that the road of the social reformer is paved

with disillusions I have determined to
rise above it.

The Noël Coward Song Book (1984)

On seeing one of these child prodigies dominate and sink
a play, despite considerable critical acclaim, Coward
remarked as he left the theatre:

Two things in that play should have been
cut. The second act and that child's
throat.

Attributed

On another occasion he was less than pleased with a child
actor's performance in a musical version of *Gone With the
Wind*. When an on-stage horse performed a natural func-
tion – perhaps in a spirit of constructive criticism –
Coward observed:

If they'd stuffed the child's head up the
horse's arse, they would have solved two
problems at once.

Another theatrical ritual that bored him was the mass
audition. Putting on one of his own revues invariably
entailed sitting in the stalls for hours on end, watching an
infinite parade of minimally talented hopefuls. One pre-
dictable mark of their lack of talent was their corre-
sponding lack of imagination when it came to choosing
their audition material. Certain items could be anticipat-
ed with ominous certainty:

The nicest words I know in the theatre are: 'That's all, sir', which signify the end of a mass audition. It means that we shan't hear 'Phil the Fluter's Ball' again that morning.

His views on what constituted good theatre were deeply held and unchanged throughout his life. Nor did he miss many opportunities to restate them:

The theatre must be treated with respect. It is a house of strange enchantment, a temple of dreams.

What it most emphatically is *not* and never will be is a scruffy, illiterate, drill-hall serving as a temporary soap-box for propaganda.

'A Warning to Actors'(1961)

★ ★ ★

I don't like propaganda in the theatre unless it is disguised so brilliantly that the audience mistakes it for entertainment. The moment the public sniffs propaganda, they stay away.

'The Art of Acting' (1961)

★ ★ ★

Consider the public. Treat it with tact and courtesy. It will accept much from you if you are clever enough to win it to your side. Never fear it or despise it. Coax it, charm it, interest it, stimulate it, shock it now and again if you must, make it laugh, make it cry and make it think, but above all... never, never, never bore the living hell out of it.

Sunday Times (1961)

★   ★   ★

To believe that public taste can be accurately assessed, even for a short period, is a dangerous illusion. Times and politics and the circumstances of living change and with them changes the public attitude to entertainment.

Play Parade Volume 4 (1954)

★   ★   ★

I have a slight reforming urge, but I have rather cunningly kept it down.

The Times (1969)

★   ★   ★

The most important ingredients of a
play are life, death, food, sex and money
– but not necessarily in that order.

★　★　★

Despite his many talents, writing plays was what he did
first and last and what he always came back to. It was his
work:

The only way to enjoy life is to work.
Work is much more fun than fun.

Observer (Sayings of the Week) (1963)

★　★　★

GARRY: If you wish to be a playwright
… go and get yourself a job as a
butler in a repertory company if
they'll have you. Learn from the
ground up how plays are constructed
and what is actable and what isn't.
Then sit down and write at least
twenty plays one after the other, and if
you can manage to get the twenty-
first produced for a Sunday night
performance you'll be damned lucky!

Present Laughter (1939)

None the less, it was a *skill* that one honed in the live theatre, not the study:

> It's no use to go and take courses in playwriting any more than it's much use taking courses in acting. Better play to a bad matinée in Hull, it will teach you much more than a year of careful instruction.
>
> Television interview (1969)

In the same interview he would add:

> Come to think of it, I never did play to a *good* matinée in Hull…

His own start had been far from stellar. On his first visit to New York in 1921 he found no one beating a path to his rented door. Finally he was offered a fee of $500 by *Metropolitan Magazine* to adapt *I'll Leave It to You* into a short story:

> I reflected gleefully that for $500 I would gladly consider turning *War and Peace* into a music-hall sketch.
>
> Present Indicative (1937)

From an early stage he was associated with the writing of comedies:

Comedy is nearly always despised in its generation and honoured more latterly – except by the public.

★ ★ ★

It's so easy to get laughs and so difficult to control them. And that's the essence of comedy.

BBC Television interview 'Great Acting' (1966)

★ ★ ★

CRESTWELL: Comedies of manners swiftly become obsolete when there are no longer any manners.

Relative Values (1951)

★ ★ ★

The critics described *Private Lives* variously as 'tenuous, thin, brittle, gossamer, iridescent and delightfully daring'. All of which connoted in the public mind cocktails, repartee and irreverent allusions to copulation, thereby causing a gratifying number of respectable people to queue up at the box office.

Play Parade Volume 1 (1934)

Sometimes he found the outcome less satisfactory. He described a 1949 revival as having 'all the chic of a whist drive in Tulse Hill' (*Diaries*).

He was also disappointed at the first-night audience's reaction to *Bitter Sweet*:

> The audience was tremendously fashionable and for the first part of the play almost as responsive as so many cornflour blancmanges.

Reflecting on the New York production of *This Was a Man*:

> The production was practically stationary. The second-act dinner scene... made *Parsifal* in its entirety seem like a quick-fire vaudeville sketch.

Wagner and his works crop up frequently in Coward's critical litany ('Not a *tremendous* Wagnerian on account of getting fidgety') and *Parsifal* came in for particular scrutiny. Having seen *Camelot* (1955):

> It's about as long as *Parsifal* and not as funny.

Coward presumably knew George Jean Nathan's crack about the work:

> It's an opera that begins at five-thirty. Three hours later you look at your watch. And it's only twenty to six.

Nor did eighteenth-century music appeal:

All too often it sounds like a Pekinese
peeing on a mink rug.
Quoted by Julian Slade

★   ★   ★

I am light-minded. I would inevitably
write a comedy if – God help me! – I
wanted to write a play with a message.

★   ★   ★

I know nothing so dreary as the feeling
that you can't make the sounds or write
the words that your whole creative being
is yearning for.
Diaries (1945)

It was his career-long dilemma that his choice of medium
tended to obscure his message:

Cocktails and laughter
But what comes after
Nobody knows
'Poor Little Rich Girl' — *On With the Dance* (1925)

Coward had no time for artistic pretension in the theatre and frequently observed that the avant-garde piece hailed by the intellectual press often failed to find comparable acclaim at the box office. This was not the route he ever intended to pursue:

I've never written for the intelligentsia. Sixteen curtain calls and closed on Saturday.

Interview with the *Daily Mirror*

★   ★   ★

I am quite prepared to admit that during my fifty-odd years of theatre-going, I have on many occasions been profoundly moved by plays about the Common Man, as in my fifty-odd years of restaurant-going I have frequently enjoyed tripe and onions, but I am not prepared to admit that an exclusive diet of either would be completely satisfying.

The Common Man, unless written or portrayed with genius, is not dramatic-ally nearly so interesting as he is claimed to be.

'A Warning to Actors' (1961)

* * *

The age of the Common Man has taken over a nation which owes its very existence to uncommon men.

Diaries (1956)

* * *

I am becoming almighty sick of the Welfare State; sick of general 'commonness', sick of ugly voices, sick of bad manners and teenagers and debased values.

Diaries (1963)

* * *

It is as dull to write incessantly about tramps and prostitutes as it is to write incessantly about dukes and duchesses and even suburban maters and paters, and it is bigoted and stupid to believe that tramps and prostitutes and underprivileged housewives frying onions and using ironing boards are automatically the salt of the earth and that nobody else is worth bothering about.

'A Warning to Pioneers' (1961)

* * *

It is true that a writer should try to hold the mirror up to nature, although there are aspects of nature that would be better unreflected.

'A Warning to Pioneers' (1961)

On the other hand, the answer was not to go to the opposite extreme of mindless froth:

I would like to prove that talent and material count for more than sequins and tits.

Referring to *Ace of Clubs* in his *Diaries* (1950)

And when it came to performing the plays:

I think the most dangerous theory advanced in modern days is that you have to feel what you do for eight performances a week. It's out of the question. And also, acting is not a state of being. Acting is acting... It's giving an impression of feeling. If it's real feeling, then you're very liable to lose your performance and lose the attention of the audience, because if you lose yourself, you're liable to lose them.

BBC Television interview 'Great Acting' (1966)

Coward was that unusual phenomenon – a playwright who also acted. Much as he adored the craft of acting, he had few illusions about some of its practitioners:

> Actors are incredibly silly, and leading ladies idiotic.

Diaries (1961)

★　★　★

> BRYAN (THE AUTHOR): Why can't people in the theatre behave like normal human beings?
> TONY (DIRECTOR'S ASSISTANT): There wouldn't be a theatre if they did.

Star Quality (unproduced play – 1967)

★　★　★

> Acting is an instinct. A gift that is often given to people who are very silly as people. But as they come on to the stage, up goes the temperature.

Advising a young actress on the need to project:

> When young I remember having a downward-looking view from the gallery of Tree and Hawtrey and I could hear every word. But now, swathed in stardom

[*19*]

in the stalls, I find I don't hear as well as in the old days.

* * *

The actor is a recollection with a lot of gold dust on it.

Advice to his fellow actors:

Speak clearly, don't bump into people, and if you must have motivation, think of your pay packet on Friday.

Speech to the Gallery First Nighters' Club (1962)

* * *

LORRAINE (THE STAR): God preserve us from enthusiastic amateurs who have ghastly theories about acting and keep on talking about rhythm and colour.

BRYAN: I thought his *Hamlet* was marvellous.

LORRAINE: All that unbleached linen and kapok. The Closet scene looked like a tea-tent.

Star Quality (unproduced play — 1967)

*Over*acting was a permanent nightmare to him. Watching Alfred Lunt at the end of *Quadrille*'s run:

> Alfred overplayed badly. He crouched and wriggled and camped about like a massive *antiquaire* in heat.

Diaries (1953)

In *Sigh No More* (1945) an enthusiastic but inexperienced young male dancer playing Harlequin had forgotten to wear his 'protector'. When he had leapt about a little, Noël instructed the choreographer, Wendy Toye:

> For God's sake, go and tell that young man to take that Rockingham tea service out of his tights.

★   ★   ★

JOANNA: I expect it's because you're an actor, they're always apt to be a bit papier mâché.

GARRY: Just puppets, Joanna dear, creatures of tinsel and sawdust, how clever of you to have noticed it.

Present Laughter (1939)

Noël's put-downs of leading ladies were legendary. In the 1964 revival of *Hay Fever* when Edith Evans consistently read the line, 'You can see as far as Marlow on a clear day' as '...on a *very* clear day', Noël corrected her with, 'No, dear, on a *very* clear day you can see Marlowe *and* Beaumont *and* Fletcher.'

At a later performance she 'took her curtain calls as though she had just been un-nailed from the cross'.

In the 1956 television version of *Blithe Spirit*, Claudette Colbert ('I'd wring her neck – if I could find it') was fluffing her lines badly:

—Oh, dear, and I knew them backwards this morning.

—And that's just the way you're delivering them, dear.

Judy Campbell was on a wartime tour of the provinces with Coward. Exasperated with what she considered his temperamental behaviour, she finally snapped:

—Oh, I could just *throw* something at you!

—Try starting with my lines.

(1943)

On Gladys Cooper's inability to remember hers in *Relative Values* (1951):

I did not expect word perfection at the first rehearsal but I had rather hoped for it on the first night.

To an actress whose first-night performance was plagued with technical problems:

> You managed to play the first act of my little comedy tonight with all the Chinese flair and light-hearted brilliance of Lady Macbeth.

Having seen the French actress Simone Signoret play Lady Macbeth in English for the first time, he summed up the production as:

> *Aimez-vous Glamis?*
>
> Washington Post (1969)

When an actress playing Queen Victoria had left Coward distinctly unamused:

> I never realised before that Albert married beneath his station.
>
> Evening Standard (1965)

★   ★   ★

> She stopped the show – but then the show wasn't really travelling very fast.

Coward once attended a session of the Actors' Studio and heard Lee Strasberg recall Eleanor Duse:

> [He] explained that when she smiled she didn't merely smile with her mouth, but

with every part of her body! Which comes under the heading of the neatest trick of the week.

Diaries (1958)

* * *

Many years ago I remember a famous actress explaining to me with perfect seriousness that before making an entrance she always stood aside and let God go on first. I can also remember that on that particular occasion He gave a singularly uninspired performance.

'Stage Fright' (1965)

* * *

Poor darling glamorous stars every-where, their lives are so lonely and wretched and frustrated. Nothing but applause, flowers, Rolls-Royces, expens-ive hotel suites, constant adulation. It's too pathetic and wrings the heart.

Diaries (1955)

* * *

Great big glamorous stars can be very
tiresome.

Diaries (1958)

★　★　★

God preserve me in future from female
stars. I don't suppose He will. I really
am too old and tired to go through all
these tired old hoops.

Diaries (1956)

But without a doubt his leading leading lady – both pro-
fessionally and personally – was Gertrud Alexandra
Dagmar Lawrence-Klausen (Gertie Lawrence). They met
as fellow child actors in 1913 and Coward recorded their
meeting in *Present Indicative*. She was, he recalled:

a vivacious child with ringlets to whom I
took an instant fancy... her face was far
from pretty, but tremendously alive. She
was very *mondaine*, carried a handbag
with a powder-puff and frequently
dabbed her generously turned-up nose.
She confided to me that her name was
Gertrude Lawrence, but that I was to
call her Gert because everybody did.

Although the names 'Noël and Gertie' became indissolubly linked, in fact they only appeared together twice as adult actors – in *Private Lives* (1930) and *Tonight at 8.30* (1936). So popular were they with the public that they talked often of the future plays he would write for the two of them. After all, there was plenty of time. Then, in 1952 – somewhere in her early fifties – Gertie died unexpectedly and Coward was asked to write her obituary in *The Times*:

> No one I have ever known, however brilliant and however gifted, has contributed quite what she contributed to my work… I wish so very deeply that I could have seen her just once more, acting in a play of mine. Her quality was, to me, unique and her magic imperishable.

Their relationship was based on their irreverent affection for each other. Even the humble telegram could be turned into a medium for wit when she was the subject. On opening in her first straight play:

LEGITIMATE AT LAST STOP WON'T MOTHER BE PLEASED

On a subsequent first night:

A WARM HAND ON YOUR OPENING

And on her 1940 marriage to Richard Aldrich:

DEAR MRS A HOORAY HOORAY
AT LAST YOU ARE DEFLOWERED
ON THIS AS EVERY OTHER DAY
I LOVE YOU NOEL COWARD

On one occasion Coward was invited to write a typical Hollywood film script to star Gertie. He replied:

REGRET CANNOT WRITE LIFE OF
SARAH BERNHARDT FOR GERTRUDE
LAWRENCE STOP TOO BUSY WRITING
LIFE OF ST TERESA FOR MAE WEST

Coward was as objective about his own stage persona as he was about other people's. Asked in a television interview if he had ever been the subject of a 'put-down', he replied:

Yes, I once left a stage door and there was a glamorous crowd welcoming me with autograph books, which I was graciously signing, when I heard someone say – 'I'll swap you three Noël Cowards for one Jessie Matthews.'

Had he ever told Miss Matthews?

Yes, she didn't speak to me for three weeks, she was so pleased with herself.

Television interview (1968)

As an actor, he was well aware of his range and the need to stay within it. Shakespeare intrigued him, and many of his plays took their titles from Shakespearian quotations – *Blithe Spirit*, *Present Laughter*, *This Happy Breed* – but to *act* the Bard was quite another matter:

I was offered Hamlet five times… I just knew that the day I declaimed 'To be or not to be' in public, it would be the death of me.

Daily Mail (1969)

Would he contemplate it in the future?

> I think I've left it a bit late! I might play
> the Nurse in *Romeo and Juliet*.

His distinctive delivery of lines became a Coward trade-mark:

> You have to hear him reciting a line like
> 'It reeks with morality' stressing the 'r's
> to make it exquisitely funny to know
> how good he can be.
>
> Critic André Senwald on the film *The Scoundrel* (1935)

In the 1950s he reinvented himself yet again as a cabaret performer:

> If it is possible to romp fastidiously, that
> is what Coward does.
>
> Kenneth Tynan reviewing his cabaret début (1951)

Although many considered him the definitive performer of his own songs, the verdict was not unanimous. A critic reviewing his 1951 cabaret début at the Café de Paris accused him of 'massacring' his material. If so, Coward declared in his *Diaries*:

> It was the most profitable massacre since
> the St. Valentine's Day massacre.

None the less, he had no illusions about his technical vocal accomplishments:

> It is a composer's voice. It has considerable range but no tone, little music, but lots of meaning.

★ ★ ★

> I can't sing but I know how to, which is quite different.

Observer (1969)

Cabaret in London and Las Vegas was to lead to television:

> The TV spectacular I am going to do with Mary Martin will be completely spontaneous. The kind of spontaneity I like best – the kind that comes after five weeks' rehearsal.

(1955)

★ ★ ★

> Time has convinced me of one thing. Television is for appearing on, not looking at.

Interview with Ed Murrow (1956)

Coward had a career-long feud with dramatic critics. Having received virtually unqualified praise in his early twenties, he found himself an early victim of media 'deconstruction' for much of the rest of his life. His crusade of retaliation didn't help matters:

> Criticism and Bolshevism have one thing in common. They both seek to pull down that which they could never build.

* * *

> I have always been fond of them [critics] … I think it is so frightfully clever of them to go night after night to the theatre and know so little about it.

* * *

> I can take any amount of criticism, so long as it is unqualified praise.
> Press interview

* * *

> If I had really cared about the critics, I would have shot myself in the Twenties.
> *Play Parade Volume 4* (1954)

* * *

> I don't know what makes them so vitriolic; I suppose it's my continued success and something about my personality that

infuriates them, in which case I fear they will have to get on with it.

Diaries (1959)

★ ★ ★

My personal attitude to the dramatic critics, after years of varying emotions, has finally solidified into an unyielding core of bored resignation.

'A Warning to Dramatic Critics' (1961)

Often the hardest part of a show was deciding what to call it. When producers Charles Russell and Lance Hamilton were looking for a name for the first of the *Night of 100 Stars* charity galas, there was a suggestion that it might be called *Summer Stars* – to which Noël quipped:

Some are not!

On another occasion the author of a new show was debating what to call it and suggested *An Enquiry into Certain Aspects of the Dogmas of World War One* – to which Coward replied:

Too snappy.

When there was some difficulty in deciding on a title for the first Coward anthology show, one of the production team suggested *Cream of Coward*. 'That would be *asking* for trouble,' Noël replied bleakly. Nevertheless, he orchestrated the dairy theme. At his suggestion the show was eventually called *Cowardy Custard* (1972).

The last show Coward ever saw was a gala performance of the compilation revue, *Oh, Coward!* Asked if he was laughing at the lines, he replied:

One doesn't laugh at his own jokes.
(1973)

During his period of dramatic apprenticeship Noël was in the habit of jotting down scraps of dialogue that might come in useful later on:

She was so *embonpoint* before her marriage that her fiancé used to use her as a cake stand.

★   ★   ★

She fell down a lift shaft on Ascension Day – so perverse of her.

★   ★   ★

—As Oscar Wilde might have said 'Golf is essentially the massive in pursuit of the minute.'
—I don't see why you should imagine the poor man would ever say anything so unfunny.

★   ★   ★

Sarcasm from you is reminiscent of a bevy of elephants leaping round a gadfly and imagining they're teasing it.

★　★　★

She's the kind of woman who only uses the Bible for blasphemous reference.

★　★　★

—Do you think a doctor would give a professional secret away?
—Of course not – honour among thieves.

★　★　★

ANGELA: On most people Christian Science has the effect of a patent egg boiler.
PAULINE: You mean it makes them hard?
ANGELA: Exactly, or so soft as to be almost unmanageable.
DENNIS: Is that in one of your novels?
ANGELA: No, but it will be.

★　★　★

Never take anything seriously, except perhaps bath salts.

★ ★ ★

My dear, there's nothing so ordinary as
to try to be extraordinary.

★ ★ ★

She didn't like mustard, otherwise she
was perfectly normal.

★ ★ ★

It was just that she had a complete set of
Ella Wheeler Wilcox that prejudiced you.

★ ★ ★

My dear, she just missed being beautiful
by buying her clothes ready-made.

★ ★ ★

She lives at Croydon and wants to see
more of life.

But perhaps the line that best sums up Coward on theatre
was this one:

If you're a star, you should behave like
one. I always have.

Sunday Times (1969)

[36]

PART TWO

—

'Mad Dogs and
Englishmen…'

★

TO THE END OF HIS DAYS Coward remained a flag-waving patriot, even if the England he celebrated had become largely a figment of his memory. In many ways he was a Victorian stranded in another era and suffering from a malaise he would term 'Twentieth Century Blues':

> *In this strange illusion,*
> *Chaos and confusion,*
> *People seem to lose their way.*
> *What is there to strive for,*
> *Love or keep alive for? Say —*
> *Hey, hey, call it a day.*
> *Blues, nothing to win or to lose.*
> *It's getting me down.*
> *Blues, I've got those weary*
>   *Twentieth Century Blues.*

'Twentieth Century Blues' – *Cavalcade* (1931)

Personally he needed to believe that the Old Country could find a new purpose. In *Cavalcade* he has the heroine (Jane Marryot), towards the end of a long life, give the New Year Toast to the Future that she has given every year:

JANE: Let's drink to the hope that one day this country of ours, which we love so much, will find dignity and greatness and peace again.

★ ★ ★

'This realm, this dear, dear land' in
which the people are sillier than ever
and the succeeding governments are also
idiotic, but my roots are sunk deep in it.

Diaries (1966)

Such overt emotion from the supposedly cynical Mr
Coward raised a number of eyebrows and questions
about his sincerity – a situation he had aggravated by his
first-night speech:

'… in spite of the troublous times we are
living in, it is still pretty exciting to be
English' … quite true, quite sincere; I
felt it strongly, but I rather wished I
hadn't said it, hadn't popped it on to the
top of *Cavalcade* like a paper-cap.

The rumour was fairly general that I
had written it with my tongue in my
cheek, probably in bed, wearing a silk
dressing-gown and shaking with cynical
laughter.

Present Indicative (1937)

For the next decade he removed his patriotism from his
sleeve, but the arrival of the Second World War changed
things. It became his ambition to write the definitive war
song – something that would match Ivor Novello's 'Keep

the Home Fires Burning' from the first 'war to end
wars'. One morning in 1941, sitting in a bomb-damaged
London railway station after a particularly bad blitz, the
sight of a small wild flower bravely struggling to survive
seemed to symbolize something about the city and the
people he loved so much:

> *London Pride has been handed down to us.*
> *London Pride is a flower that's free.*
> *London Pride means our own dear town to us,*
> *And our pride it forever will be...*
> *Cockney feet*
> *Mark the beat of history.*
> *Every street*
> *Pins a memory down.*
> *Nothing ever can quite replace*
> *The grace of London Town.*
> 'London Pride' (1941)

It was a sentiment he was to express in words (and often music) for the next thirty years:

> *London — is a little bit of all right,*
> *Nobody can deny that's true . . .*
> *London — is a place where you can call right*
> *Round and have a cosy cup of tea,*
> *If you're fed right up and got your tail*
>   *right down*
> *London town*
> *Is a wonderful place to be.*
>
> London sequence – *The Girl Who Came to Supper* (1963)

Perhaps, though, there were one or two small improvements we could make:

> *We downtrodden British must learn to*
>   *be skittish*
> *And give an impression of devil-may-*
>   *care . . .*
>
> 'Don't Make Fun of the Fair' (The 1951 Festival of Britain was designed to raise post-war morale)

As the years went by, though, he found it progressively harder to equate Swinging Sixties England with the *Great Britain* he had known. In 1963 he attended the annual Battle of Britain dinner and found himself asking:

> What was it that I so minded about twenty-three years ago? An ideal? An

abstract patriotism? What?... I wanted suddenly to stand up and shout... 'Let's face the truth. The England we knew and loved was betrayed at Munich, revived for one short year in 1940 and was supreme in adversity, and now no longer exists.' That last great war was our valediction. It will never happen again.

Diaries (1963)

★   ★   ★

I continue to tell foreigners how great we are. Before I die, I would like once again to be able to believe this myself.

Sunday Express (1965)

Like any good Englishman, Coward was perfectly well aware that the rest of the world found us perplexing, to say the least. His attitude was: but then, they were, were they not – *foreigners*? How could they be expected to understand?

> *It's such a surprise for the Eastern eyes*
>   *to see*
> *That though the English are effete,*
> *They're quite impervious to heat,*
> *When the white man rides every native*
>   *hides in glee,*

Because the simple creatures hope he
Will impale his solar topee on a tree...
It seems such a shame
When the English claim
The earth
That they give rise to such hilarity
and mirth.

'Mad Dogs and Englishmen' (1930)

And they did, after all, look pretty strange to us:

We British are an island race,
The sea lies all around us,
And visitors from other lands,
With different sets of different glands,
Bewilder and astonish us.

Conversation Piece (1934)

There was our age-old sparring partner across the Channel:

There's always something fishy about
the French!
We've a sinister suspicion
That behind their savoir-faire
They share
A common contempt
For every mother's son of us.

Tho' they smile and smirk
We know they're out for dirty work...
Every wise and thoroughly worldly wench
Knows there's always something fishy
about the French!

Conversation Piece (1934)

Although we may not be entirely blameless ourselves:

> *Foreigners' immorality may make us look*
> *   askance,*
> *Though we are not above it if we get the*
> *   slightest chance.*
> *What is it makes an Englishman enjoy*
> *   himself in France?*

Or, if you looked across that other stretch of sea:

> The Irish behave exactly as they have
> been portrayed as behaving for years.
> Charming, soft-voiced, quarrelsome,
> priest-ridden, feckless and happily
> devoid of integrity in our stodgy English
> sense of the word.

Then, of course, there were the Germans. Coward's side-swipe at them early in the war was totally misread by many and censored for a while until the irony was firmly established. An exception was Winston Churchill who 'liked it so much that I had to sing it to him seven times in one evening'.

> *Don't let's be beastly to the Germans*
> *When the age of peace and plenty has begun.*
> *We must send them steel and oil and coal*
> *   and everything they need*

For their peaceable intentions can be always
    guaranteed.
Let's employ with them a sort of 'strength
    through joy' with them,
They're better than us at honest manly fun.
Let's let them feel they're swell again and
    bomb us all to hell again,
But don't let's be beastly to the Hun.

'Don't Let's Be Beastly to the Germans' (1943)

* * *

The Germans have been aggressive,
cruel and humourless all through their
dismal history, and I find it quite impos-
sible to forgive them, however politic it
may be considered to do so. They are a
horrid, neurotic race and always have
been and always will be and, to my mind,
none of their contributions to science,
literature and music compensates for
their turgid emotionalism and unpar-
alleled capacity for torturing their
fellow creatures.

Diaries (1955)

* * *

There is, alas, no new *Cavalcade* to be
written. Oh dear, no. A *Cavalcade* of
Germany perhaps, or Japan. They are
countries of industry and determination.
We, alas, were victors and there is little
more demoralizing than that, it seems.

Diaries (1956)

The Austrians, on the other hand, he always found to be
'sweet people but overmusical':

*When we wake in the morning, the very first
thing
That we Austrians do is to sing and to sing.
Tho' on every occasion our voices excel
In a National crisis we yodel as well.*

Operette (1938)

★   ★   ★

*Having been deafened by Wagnerian
bassoons
I much prefer these ultra-British
Rather skittish
Little tunes*

Unpublished song – *The Girl Who Came to Supper* (1962)

Most other parts of the world, it seems, he could take or
leave:

Saint Petersburg, of course, has flair
But can be dull without the snow,
Berlin is much too polyglot
And Rome in summer is dreadfully hot,
Vienna makes one ill at ease
With those vocal Viennese,
And Athens with its ruins and fleas
Is far too Greek.

Unpublished song – *After the Ball* (1953)

★   ★   ★

SHOLTO: There's always a political crisis in Bulgaria, the same as there's always haggis in Scotland. It's traditional.

The Young Idea (1921)

★   ★   ★

They all insist that South America's exotic
Whereas it couldn't be more boring if it tried.

'Nina' (1945)

The one place that fascinated and frustrated him in equal measure from his first sight of it in 1921 was America:

I like America,
I have played around
Every slappy-happy hunting ground

[49]

But I find America — okay...
I like America,
Every scrap of it,
All the sentimental crap of it.
'I Like America' — *Ace of Clubs* (1949)

But while he might like *America*, he never ceased to be amazed at the more bizarre aspects of Americans and Americana in general:

I love the weight of American Sunday newspapers. Pulling them up off the floor is good for the figure.

★   ★   ★

Without America we should have no Coca-Cola, no Marilyn Monroe and hardly any really good literature about sex.
Attributed

★   ★   ★

American women mostly have their clothes arranged for them. And their faces, too, I think.

★   ★   ★

Americans love ice and hate cold water and so the swimming pools are as hot as *bouillabaisse*.

★   ★   ★

It is really surprising how many American adults... have plunged into psychiatry so that their egos have grown inwards, like toenails.

Diaries (1962)

★   ★   ★

I hate the United States' behaviour to English, with such words as 'hospitalized' and 'togetherness'. And how about 'trained nurse'? Absurd. What in heaven's name is the use of an *un*trained nurse?

★   ★   ★

MELODY: Americans have a passion for speed... and yet no idea of time whatsoever – it's most extraordinary.

★   ★   ★

LINDSAY: Norma's always had English cigarettes since the Prince of Wales came to America in nineteen whatever it was.
CHUCK: Did she meet him?
LINDSAY: I don't think so but there

was always the chance that his car
might have broken down nearby when
he was on his way to somewhere else.

Time Remembered (unproduced play – 1941)

★   ★   ★

MAXIE: Buffet lunches… are always a
drain on one's vitality. They call them
fork luncheons over here, you know. I
always think it sounds vaguely porno-
graphic.

Time Remembered (unproduced play – 1941)

PART THREE

'The Stately Homes of England'

★

THE ENGLISH CLASS SYSTEM was a recurrent theme in Coward's work. Although his own origins were lower-middle class, the public persona he created enabled him to mingle with all levels of society and his perception ensured that he saw all of its strata clearly and took none of them entirely seriously.

There was, for example, the Landed Gentry:

> *The Stately Homes of England,*
> *How beautiful they stand,*
> *To prove the upper classes*
> *Have still the upper hand;*
> *Though the fact that they have to be rebuilt*
> *And frequently mortgaged to the hilt*
> *Is inclined to take the gilt*
> *Off the gingerbread...*

'The Stately Homes of England' – *Operette* (1938)

★ ★ ★

AMANDA: Whose yacht is that?
ELYOT: The Duke of Westminster's I expect. It always is.

Private Lives (1930)

But there was aristocracy and aristocracy. Observing a mixed bag of minor honourables at a society wedding long after the Royals had departed, Coward remarked to a fellow guest, Richard Burton:

Here come the riff-raff.

And then, of course, there were the poor Rich...
Considering his friends, the Westminsters:

Stone walls do not a prison make nor
iron bars a cage, but millions of pounds
can make, very subtly, both.
(1962)

During his lifetime, Coward's beady eye was always busy
'watching Society scampering past' and observing its
mores shift. In the 1920s it was perfectly permissible –
even *de rigueur* – to appear socially frivolous:

EUSTACE: The only thing more expens-
ive than hunting is virtue.

The Young Idea (1921)

★   ★   ★

CICELY: I do wish you wouldn't despise
my husband so, Roddy, it isn't good form.

The Young Idea (1921)

★   ★   ★

JENNIFER: I have never been able to
take anything seriously after eleven
o'clock in the morning.

The Young Idea (1921)

★   ★   ★

If it's rissoles, I shan't dress – a rule I
made in 1929 and to which I still strictly
adhere.

And the world could safely be populated with social but-
terflies and chinless wonders – a species that could still
be occasionally sighted years later. Coward recalled
meeting 'a startled young man fresh from Oxford with
over-eager teeth' as late as 1953 (*Diaries*).

The war, though, had changed all that and the values
of the post-war world were not particularly to Coward's
liking:

FELICITY: One of the worst aspects of modern English life is that so many of one's friends have to work and they're so bad at it.

Relative Values (1951)

★   ★   ★

CRESTWELL (THE BUTLER): Above all I drink to the final inglorious disintegration of the most unlikely dream that ever troubled the foolish heart of man – Social Equality!

Relative Values (1951)

There were – or should be – certain fixed points even in a changing world and over the years Coward would seek to define them:

Manners are the outward expression of expert interior decoration.

Long Island Sound (unproduced play — 1947)

On taste:

It can be vulgar, but it must never be embarrassing.

★   ★   ★

Style in everything demands discipline.
Daily Mail (1966)

★   ★   ★

Conceit is an outward manifestation
of inferiority.
(1969)

★   ★   ★

I absolutely loathe champagne. Have
since I was twenty.
New York Herald Tribune (1963)

When you come right down to it, he concluded quite
early, each of us had to decide who we wanted to be and
then set about creating that persona. He certainly devoted his own life to doing so:

LEO: It's all a question of masks, really;
brittle, painted masks. We all wear
them as a form of protection; modern
life forces us to. We must have some
means of shielding our timid,
shrinking souls from the glare of
civilization.
Design for Living (1932)

Of course, for the true Social Animal, a certain amount
of civilized glare was inevitable. After all, there were the

inevitable parties to go to... and one in particular. Coward never forgot the 1930s party in the south of France to which hostess Elsa Maxwell invited him. When he arrived, he found that he was expected to entertain the guests. He firmly declined, then enshrined the occasion in song:

I went to a marvellous party,
We played the most wonderful game,
Maureen disappeared
And came back in a beard
And we all had to guess at her name!
We talked about growing old gracefully
And Elsie who's seventy-four
Said, 'A, it's a question of being sincere,
And B, if you're supple you've nothing to fear.'
Then she swung upside down from a glass
  chandelier,
I couldn't have liked it more.

'I Went to a Marvellous Party' — *Set to Music* (1939)

By comparison, subsequent parties often lacked a certain *je ne sais quoi*:

Larry Harvey was 'in a Rodin *penseur* mood' and the Henry Fondas 'lay on the evening like a damp mackintosh'.

Diaries (1960)

[60]

★   ★   ★

It was a nice party, except for Joan
Fontaine's titties which kept falling
about and a large rock python which was
handed to me as a surprise.

Coward's description of a 1948 Hollywood party

Though he was a regular visitor from the early 1930s, the
movie capital never really attracted him:

I'm not very keen on Hollywood… I'd
rather have a nice cup of cocoa, really.

Letter to his mother (1931)

And as the cocktails flowed at every social occasion
worth the name, the talk would inevitably turn to The
Arts. No matter what the year, there was the endless
debate over the Modern Novel:

MRS ASTON-HOOPER: I get so tired of
the usual modern novels. They nearly
always end with the hero having been
married forty years to the heroine,
gazing down the vista of his life and
saying – 'I wonder', until a dotted line
cuts his rather aimless musings short.

The Unattainable (unpublished play — 1918)

★   ★   ★

BOBBIE: I've read the modern novelists
and I *know*; all you do is walk about
with arms entwined, and write poems
of tigerish adoration to your mistress.
It's a beautiful existence.

I'll Leave It to You (1919)

Whatever he chose to say in his plays, in private life he
was positively puritanical:

If there's anything I hate in modern
novels it is this sex obsession, this pseudo-
tough realism in which every sexual
depravity is intimately dissected. It drags
one straight back to Jane Austen.

Interview (1968)

★   ★   ★

A modern novel can be forgiven
anything providing it is long enough.

Cole Lesley — *Remembered Laughter* (1976)

Then there was Art – both Ancient, as on seeing the
Venus de Milo:

It's only what's to be expected if you
will go on biting your nails.

... and Modern (a particular Coward *bête noire*):

SEBASTIEN: I don't think anyone knows
about painting any more. Art, like
human nature, has got out of hand.

Nude with Violin (1954)

After reading Wilenski's book *Lives of the Impressionists*:

Really no burlesque however extrava-
gant could equal the phrases he uses to
describe the 'Abstract' boys. Quite a lot
of it is completely unintelligible. He
talks a great deal of 'emotive force' and
'lyrical colour' and 'constant functional
forms', etc., and after he has described
a picture in approximately these terms
you turn to a coloured plate and look at
a square lady with three breasts and a
guitar up her crotch.

Diaries (1954)

★   ★   ★

He's running a temperature and his
chest looks like a bad Matisse.

Pomp and Circumstance (1960)

Society did a lot of 'scampering past' during Coward's
lifetime and, after the initial sense of loss, he was inclined
to wonder whether, after all, nostalgia was quite what it
used to be:

It was a *nostalgie du temps perdu* and I
wasn't somehow all that sorry when the
temps were *perdu*.

Diaries (1966)

★   ★   ★

It is a natural enough malaise, this
idealised remembering, but should not
be encouraged too much. There is no
future in the past.

Diaries (1954)

TRAVEL WAS COWARD's safety valve. When his pressured professional life caught up with him – which it frequently did – his recourse was to embark on a long trip to recharge his batteries.

> *When the storm clouds are riding through a*
> >   *winter sky*
> *Sail away – sail away.*
> *When the love-light is fading in your*
> >   *sweetheart's eye*
> *Sail away – sail away.*
> *When you feel your song is orchestrated wrong*
> *Why should you prolong*
> *Your stay?*
> *When the wind and the weather blow your*
> >   *dreams sky high*
> *Sail away – sail away – sail away!*
> 'Sail Away' *Ace of Clubs* (1950)

Much of his best work was done on the road to Samarkand (or somewhere similar).

> *I travel alone*
> *Sometimes I'm East,*
> *Sometimes I'm West,*
> *No chains can ever bind me;*
> *No remembered love can ever find me;*
> *I travel alone.*
> 'I Travel Alone' (1930)

The romantic in him liked to depict himself as the lone wanderer, the Flying Englishman. The more mundane truth is that he rarely travelled alone but generally with one or more members of his loyal 'family'.

I love to go and I love to have been, but best of all I love the intervals between arrivals and departures.

Present Indicative (1937)

★   ★   ★

I love travelling, but I'm always too late or too early. I arrive in Japan when the cherry blossoms have fallen. I get to China too early for the next revolution. I reach Canada when the maple leaves have gone. People are always telling me about something I haven't seen. I find it very pleasant.

Diaries (1965)

★   ★   ★

AMANDA: And India, the burning Ghars, or Ghats, or whatever they are, and the Taj Mahal. How *was* the Taj Mahal?… And it didn't look like a biscuit box, did it? I've always felt that it might.

Private Lives (1930)

★ ★ ★

I have not, as yet, seen the Taj Mahal at all, but I feel that when I do it will probably lie down in a consciously alluring attitude and pretend to be asleep.

Present Indicative (1937)

Travelling hopefully, however, had its downside. Having slept uncomfortably in a hotel bed in the tropics, he was asked by the Manager if the hotel could put up a sign to say 'Noël Coward Slept Here'. He replied:

If you'll add one word – 'Fitfully'.

★   ★   ★

I wonder who thought of introducing leatherette into the tropics? Whoever did should have his balls snipped off and fastened to his nose with a safety pin. This should also happen to whoever thought of leatherette in the first place.

Diaries (1968)

Reflecting on a 1944 African trip:

The Dinkas' claim to fame is that they are very tall, have the longest penises in the world and dye their hair with urine; doubtless cause and effect.

Future Indefinite (1954)

★   ★   ★

A: No hard liquor. It's a rule I learned in the tropics.
B: Which tropics?
A: Palm Beach.

Long Island Sound (unproduced play — 1947)

Once again, the telegram provided a concise form of communication with his nearest and dearest:

HAVE MOVED HOTEL EXCELSIOR
STOP COUGHING MYSELF INTO
A FIRENZE

Telegram from Florence
Cole Lesley — *Remembered Laughter* (1976)

On another occasion he wired:

AM BACK FROM ISTANBUL WHERE
I WAS KNOWN AS ENGLISH
DELIGHT

Telegram to Cole Lesley

An ardent visitor, Coward was a less enthusiastic host. If a guest was welcome for a return engagement, he or she would be played out of the house with a recording of 'I'll See You Again'.

The most beautiful thing about having people to stay is when they leave.

Volcano (unpublished play — 1957)

On his travels Coward was increasingly appalled by the mind and manners of his fellow travellers. In *Suite in Three Keys* (1965) an American lady tourist is complaining to another about her husband's lack of enthusiasm for seeing the sights:

I managed to drag him into Saint Peter's in Rome and all he did was stomp

around humming 'I Like New York in
June' under his breath. I was mortified.

Exposure to a travelling lifetime of such incidents finally
caused him to ask:

> *Why do the wrong people travel, travel,*
>   *travel,*
> *When the right people stay back home?*
> *What explains this mass mania*
> *To leave Pennsylvania*
> *And clack around like flocks of geese,*
> *Demanding dry martinis on the Isles of*
>   *Greece?*

'Why Do the Wrong People Travel?' — *Sail Away* (1961)

And his final verdict on the world according to Coward?

My body has certainly wandered a good
deal, but I have an uneasy suspicion that
my mind has not wandered nearly
enough.

Present Indicative (1937)

PART FIVE

—

'If Love Were All…'

★

COWARD'S IMAGE seemed to suggest that the brittle should predominate over the more sensitive emotions, yet, when asked for the one word which encapsulated his life, he was in no doubt. Nor did he seek to wrap it in an aphorism: 'LOVE'. Throughout his life he was alternately a willing and an unwilling victim of it and he found fame no defence against its slings and arrows. He summed it up most personally, perhaps, through Manon, the cabaret singer:

> *I believe in doing what I can,*
> *In crying when I must,*
> *In laughing when I choose.*
> *Heigh-ho, if love were all*
> *I should be lonely…*
>
> *But I believe that since my life began*
> *The most I've had is just*
> *A talent to amuse*
> *Heigh-ho, if love were all!*
>
> 'If Love Were All' – *Bitter Sweet* (1929)

★ ★ ★

To love and be loved is the most important thing in the world but it is often
painful.

(1950)

★ ★ ★

How idiotic people are when they're in love. What an age-old devastating disease.

Cole Lesley – *Remembered Laughter* (1976)

★　★　★

To me, passionate love has always been like a tight shoe rubbing blisters on my Achilles heel…

Diaries (1957)

★   ★   ★

Love is a true understanding of just a
few people for each other. Passionate
love we will leave on one side for that
rises, gets to its peak and dies away. True
love is something much more akin to
friendship and friendship, I suppose, is
the greatest benison and compensation
that Man has.

(1970)

But, then, there was Love and there was Marriage – an
altogether more questionable enterprise. On that subject
– never having tried it – Coward was (at least in print) of
one mind:

OLIVE: Marriage nowadays is nothing
but a temporary refuge for those who
are uncomfortable at home.

The Rat Trap (1918)

On marriage:

There are many reasons why you should
marry – for love or for money – and
many why you shouldn't.

★   ★   ★

Table d'hôte is marriage.
Free love is à la carte.

★　★　★

She married in haste and repented at Brixton.

Line of unused dialogue (*c.* 1918)

★　★　★

ZOE: I must say I consider marriage an overrated amusement.

This Was a Man (1926)

★　★　★

TOBY: Marriage is a sacrament, a mystic rite, and you persist in regarding it as a sort of plumber's estimate.

Ways and Means (1935)

The simple fact of life for Coward was that men and women were two entirely different species, fundamentally incompatible and not meant to live together:

ELYOT: It doesn't suit women to be promiscuous.

AMANDA: It doesn't suit men for women to be promiscuous.

Private Lives (1930)

★ ★ ★

RUTH: Your view of women is academic
to say the least of it — just because
you've always been dominated by them
it doesn't necessarily follow that you
know anything about them.

Blithe Spirit (1941)

★ ★ ★

I have drunk from the Well of Truth and
I feel it incumbent upon me to say that
no man could possibly go on loving you
after he had seen you in curlers.

Line of unused dialogue (c. 1919)

★ ★ ★

SHOLTO: I don't think one *could* go too
far with Priscilla. She has no distance.

The Young Idea (1921)

★ ★ ★

SANDRA: Poor Cuckoo... She's not bad
once you get below the surface.
BOFFIN: I'll wear an aqua-lung.

South Sea Bubble (1949)

★ ★ ★

SHOLTO: Did you enjoy your dance
with him?

GERDA: Awfully. His hands were like
wet hot-water bottles.

The Young Idea (1921)

* * *

STELLA: I always had my suspicions
about Derek. There was something
about the way he played the piano.

Age Cannot Wither (unproduced play – 1967)

* * *

ELYOT: Certain women should be
struck regularly, like gongs.

Private Lives (1930)

* * *

JUDITH: I detest her. She's far too old
for you, and she goes about using Sex
as a sort of shrimping-net.

Hay Fever (1924)

* * *

IRIS: I like men who go about a bit and
see life.

LADY CARRINGTON: I suppose that's

why so many women marry commercial
travellers.

The Unattainable (unproduced play – 1918)

★   ★   ★

— I don't think my husband's been
entirely faithful to me.
— Whatever makes you think that?
— My last child doesn't resemble him in
the slightest.

This Year of Grace! (1928)

★   ★   ★

SANDRA: Nothing has ever been able to
   convince the Samoans that sex is
   wrong. To them it's just as simple as
   eating mangoes.
BOFFIN: Only less stringy and indigest-
   ible.

South Sea Bubble (1949)

Garry Essendine on sex:

To me the whole business is vastly overrated. I enjoy it for what it's worth and
fully intend to go on doing so for as long
as anybody's interested and when the

[*81*]

time comes that they're not I shall be
perfectly content to settle down with an
apple and a good book!

Present Laughter (1939)

In his personal life Coward adored women and wrote
most of his greatest parts for them. None the less,
throughout his career they were perpetual targets of his
pen:

I can't think of one beautiful historical
lady in a position of power who wasn't a
dithering idiot. I suppose it's the beauty
that does it. Oh, for the humour and
horse-sense of Queen Elizabeth I. I have
a feeling that Boadicea might have been
fairly bright but they were neither of
them Gladys Coopers.

(1967)

Although he was perceptive in writing about women in
his plays, some of his private musings would hardly have
appealed to the Feminist Movement:

Imagine the chaos that would ensue if
our destinies were ruled, even tempor-
arily, by Nancy Astor or Clare Booth
Luce! Beatrice Lillie would be infinitely

less perilous. Some day I must really
settle down to writing a biography of
that arch-idiot Joan of Arc.

Diaries (1967)

★ ★ ★

JENNIFER: Isn't Marie attractive? She
has no morals and many more children
than are usual for a single woman.

The Young Idea (1921)

★ ★ ★

ERIC: I don't think women ought to go
on being vulnerable after forty. It
diminishes them.

Star Quality (unproduced play — 1967)

★   ★   ★

[She] was one of those ladies who seem
to prefer Saks to sex.

Line of unused dialogue (1950s)

Not that male weakness fared any better:

> *Every peach out of reach is attractive*
> *'Cos it's just a little bit too high,*
> *And you'll find that every man*
> *Will try to pluck it if he can*
> *As he passes by.*
> *For the brute loves the fruit that's forbidden*
> *And I'll bet you half a crown*
> *He'll appreciate the flavour of it much,*
>   *much more*
> *If he has to climb a bit to shake it down.*

'Forbidden Fruit' (1915)

Noël later commented:

True, the suggested wager of half a
crown rather lets down the tone. One

[*84*]

cannot help feeling that a bet of fifty
pounds, or at least a fiver, would be more
in keeping with the general urbanity of
the theme… but this perhaps is hyper-
criticism and it must also be remembered that to the author half a crown in
1916 was the equivalent of five pounds
in 1926. Also, it rhymes with 'down'.

Present Indicative (1937)

Nor did time improve matters:

> *Time and again*
> *I'm tortured by contrition*
> *And swear that I'm sorry I've sinned,*
> *Then when I've lashed myself with whips*
>   *and scourges*
> *Sex emerges,*
> *Out pop all the urges.*
> 'Time and Again' (1955)

★ ★ ★

> *Sex and champagne as social institutions*
> *Stampede me*
> *And lead me astray*
> 'Time and Again' (1955)

★ ★ ★

[85]

Freud could explain my curious condition
And Jung would have certainly grinned.
When I meet some sly dish
Who looks like my dish
I'm drunk — sunk — gone with the wind.
'Time and Again' (1955)

★   ★   ★

CHARLES: It's discouraging to think how
many people are shocked by honesty
and how few by deceit.
Blithe Spirit (1941)

In cynical mood even sex was not all it was cracked up
to be:

Travellers' cheques can
Do more than sex can...
'You're a Long, Long Way from America' — *Sail Away* (1961)

★   ★   ★

I think sex is overrated practically
everywhere – and sometimes
underrated. There is far too much
nonsense talked about it.
(1969)

As far as his own contribution to the Battle of the Sexes
was concerned:

[86]

I am the world's sexiest man... Indeed,
if I put my mind to it, I am sure I could
pass the supreme test and lure Miss
Taylor away from Mr Burton.

Noël was once being conducted around the red-light district of Honolulu:

... when to my great surprise from an
upstairs room in a down-at-the-heel
bordello I heard the sound of my own
voice singing – 'London Pride has been
handed down to us...' I didn't think I'd
be all that much of a come-on – but
apparently I am!

Television interview with David Frost (1969)

But – as was so often the case – the deeper feelings were
left to the privacy of verse:

I'll see you again,
Whenever spring breaks through again;
Time may lie heavy between,
But what has been
Is past forgetting.

'I'll See You Again' – *Bitter Sweet* (1929)

★   ★   ★

[87]

Time and tide can never sever
Those whom love has bound forever
'Lover of My Dreams' – *Cavalcade* (1931)

★　★　★

I'm no good at love
I betray it with little sins
For I feel the misery of the end
In the moment that it begins
And the bitterness of the last good-bye
Is the bitterness that wins.
'I'm No Good at Love' – *Not Yet the Dodo* (1967)

PART SIX

'The Party's Over Now...'

★

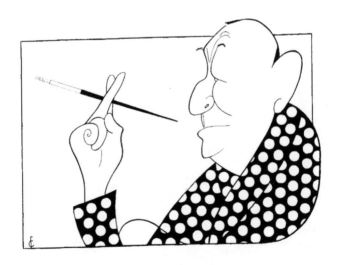

MANY PEOPLE are surprised to find that religion – how-ever disorganized – was a thread that ran through Coward's life. His attitude to it was at best ambivalent but, like a spiritual itch, he kept scratching it:

> *Do I believe in God?*
> *Well, yes, I suppose in a sort of way*
> *It's really terribly hard to say.*

'Do I Believe?' – *Collected Verse* (1984)

His first exposure was early. As a nine-year-old child per-former he was asked to sing anthems in churches:

> But I hated doing this because the lack of applause depressed me. It irritated me when I had soared magnificently through 'God is a Spirit' or 'Oh, for the Wings of a Dove' to see the entire congregation scuffle on to their knees murmuring gloomy 'Amens' instead of clapping loudly and shouting 'Bravo'.

Present Indicative (1937)

At sixteen the contact with religion was rather more per-sonal. In a 1969 television interview he told David Frost how at his Confirmation class the local Vicar had touched his knee, causing Coward to remark:

> Vicar, you are supposed to be preparing me for Confirmation. When I have

received the gift of the Holy Spirit, if
I'm in the mood, I'll telephone you.

Nor was this to be his only brush with the Church (so to
speak). When the local vicar called at his Kent home early
in 1946:

He talked a great deal of cock and never
drew breath. Matelot [Coward's dog]
complicated the interview by attempting
to rape him. I removed him saying —
'Matelot, *not* the vicar!'

Diaries (1946)

Although he could reflect on God in the privacy of his
Diaries or in verse, he became self-conscious when the
subject cropped up in public. In the interview with Frost
he was asked about his attitude to God:

We've never been intimate — but maybe
we do have a few things in common.

... and when Frost pressed him on his personal visions of
Hell:

They're all to do with over-acting!
(1969)

Nor was he averse to invoking the Deity on really important occasions. For instance, the afternoon nap was
sacrosanct. He told Cole Lesley, his chief aide:

If God rings, tell Him I'm not in.

Cole Lesley – *Remembered Laughter* (1976)

★   ★   ★

LADY CARRINGTON: Prayer only
   becomes really trying when one has
   linoleum in one's bedroom.

The Unattainable (unpublished play – 1918)

★   ★   ★

I do not care for any church, not even
the dear old Mother Church. I do not
believe there is a Universal Truth and, if
you've found it, you're a better man
than I am, Gunga Din.

Television interview (1970)

★   ★   ★

Christianity has caused a great deal more
suffering both mentally and physically,
than any other religion in the history of
mankind.

Diaries (1955)

The Servants of the Lord came in for their share of gentle
mockery. In the song 'I Wonder What Happened to Him',
Cyril Ritchard had trouble with the lines:

Whatever became of old Keeling?
I hear that he got back from France
And frightened three nuns in a train in
    Darjeeling
By stripping and waving his lance!
Sigh No More (1945)

When questioned by Noël he scrambled together the excuse that he had an aunt who was a nun. After a moment's thought, Noël replied, 'Oh, very well, then – make it *four* nuns.'

'Morality' was not the word that leapt immediately to mind in conversations about Coward and yet he wrote *The Vortex*, he said, out of a 'moral impetus'. So what, asked David Frost, do you do with your moral impetus nowadays?

I give it a little groundsel and feed it gently – it does all right.

Television interview (1970)

★　★　★

You'll grow out of it, dear, it's only a passing phase like thrush or measles. Girls always begin with religious mania, then become atheists and after that agnostics. When these three milestones are past, one can comfortably expect to settle down.

Line of unused dialogue (*c.*1918)

★　★　★

Astrology. I wasn't passionately interested in whether I was a Sagittarius or Taurus. I thought I was just *me*. Which is a very Sagittarian thing to say.

In his writings – often through the mouths of his characters – he would speculate on the Great Mysteries of the Universe:

CHARLES: Life without faith is an arid business.

Blithe Spirit (1941)

★ ★ ★

LEO: Life is a pleasure trip… a Cheap Excursion.

Design for Living (1932)

★ ★ ★

Tout lasse, tout passe, tout casse. Life goes on and little bits of us get lost.

Diaries (1957)

★ ★ ★

MADAME ARCATI: Time is the reef upon which all our frail mystic ships are wrecked.

Blithe Spirit (1941)

★ ★ ★

Time, as I have so often wittily said, is a great healer.

Diaries (1963)

★ ★ ★

ELYOT: Death's very laughable, such a cunning little mystery. All done with mirrors.

Private Lives (1930)

* * *

Old age is cruel and death much kinder when it is gentle.

Diaries (1953)

* * *

Cole (Lesley) and I had a long and cosy talk about death the other evening... we came to the sensible conclusion that there was nothing to be done. We should have to get on with life until our time came. I said, 'After all, the day had to go on and breakfast had to be eaten', and he replied that if I died he might find it a little difficult to eat breakfast but would probably be peckish by lunch-time.

Diaries (1961)

* * *

Personally I wish only for ultimate oblivion, which is fortunate because I think it is all I shall get... Why not get on with

the material and experience at hand and
try to make the best of it?... I am neither
impressed by, nor frightened of, death. I
admit that I am scared about the manner
of my dying.

Diaries (1955)

★ ★ ★

Caricature by William Auerbach-Levy

I would prefer Fate to allow me to go to
sleep when it's my proper bedtime. I never
have been one for staying up too late.
Diaries (1967)

★   ★   ★

The human race is cruel, idiotic, sentimental, predatory, ungrateful, ugly,
conceited and egocentric to the last
ditch and the occasional discovery of
an isolated exception is as deliciously
surprising as finding a sudden Brazil nut
in what you *know* to be five pounds of
vanilla creams.

By the mid-1950s Coward was less worried about a visit
from the Grim Reaper than the possibility of a 'great big
hydrogen war'. In which case:

I shall retire here [Jamaica] with as many
loved ones as I can persuade to join me
and hope for the best, eat yams and pray
that the sea doesn't become radioactive
enough to bugger up the fish… I intend
to survive, if possible, and lay in a lot of
Worcester sauce… and books and paints
and writing paper. I shall also lay in

toilet paper, the *Encyclopaedia Britannica*, a donkey and cart, and a lot of tinned soup.

Diaries (1955)

The young Coward must have felt himself to be immortal but, as with everyone, the passing years took their toll, and age became a recurrent topic:

Time's wingèd chariot is beginning to goose me.

Diaries (1959)

★   ★   ★

An old boarding-house is not going to be the last ditch.

★   ★   ★

It is said that old age has its compensations. I wonder what they are?

Diaries (1967)

His advice to Edith Evans:

If a person over fifty tries too hard to be 'with it', they soon find they're without everything.

Attributed

Trying to talk to Marlene Dietrich on the subject of old age:

I said to her, with an effort at grey
comedy, 'All I demand from my friends
nowadays is that they live through lunch,'
to which she replied, puzzled, 'Why
lunch, sweetheart?'

Diaries (1968)

On his sixty-ninth birthday:

I sat up in bed submerged in [gift]
wrappings and looking like an ancient
Buddhist priest with a minor attack of
jaundice. One year off seventy now!
Just fancy. The snows of yesteryear are
a bloody long way off.

Diaries (1968)

None the less, he did find compensations – in the love of
'family' and friends:

When I have fears, as Keats had fears,
Of the moment I'll cease to be
I console myself with vanished years
Remembered laughter, remembered tears,
And the peace of the changing sea.

Collected Verse (1984)

★　★　★

We shall still be together
When our life's journey ends,
For wherever we chance to go
We shall always be friends.
We may find while we're travelling
*   through the years*
Moments of joy and love and happiness.
Reason for grief, reason for tears.
Come the wild, wild weather,
If we've lost or we've won,
We'll remember these words we say
Till our story is done.

'Come the Wild, Wild Weather' (1960)

★   ★   ★

I do not approve of mourning, I approve only of remembering.

—

PART SEVEN

Envoi:
'I'll See You Again...'
(Coward on Coward)

★

COWARD'S OWN best invention was himself. As the years went by he got into the habit of reviewing himself as though he were a character in one of his own plays – and, indeed, without too much of a stretch, he is to be found lurking inside certain of them. Garry Essendine in *Present Laughter* (1939) is perhaps the most obvious, and demonstrates the apparent paradox between the shy man and the show-off:

GARRY: I don't give a hoot about posterity. Why should I worry about what people think of me when I'm dead as a doornail anyway? My worst defect is that I am apt to worry too much about what people think of me when I'm alive.

Present Laughter (1939)

Looking back on his life Coward could conclude:

First I was the *enfant terrible*. Then the Bright Young Thing. Now I'm a tradition.

Humble origins were most definitely *de rigueur* as the basis for a dramatic life:

> I was truculent apparently about being born and made, with my usual theatrical acumen, a delayed entrance.
>
> *Diaries* (1954)

★   ★   ★

> Oh, how fortunate I was to be born poor. If mother had been able to afford to send me to private school, Eton and Oxford or Cambridge, it would probably have set me back years.
>
> *Diaries* (1967)

★   ★   ★

> I know a great deal more about the hearts and minds of ordinary South Londoners than they [the critics] gave me credit for. My metamorphosis into a 'Mayfair Play-boy' many years later was entirely a journalistic conception.
>
> *Play Parade Volume 4* (1954)

As it was he gave the journalists a helping hand in the shaping of the appropriate persona, and charted not only where he intended to go but how to get there:

I am determined to travel through life
first class.

★ ★ ★

I have always prided myself on my
capacity for being just one jump ahead
of what everybody expects of me.

★ ★ ★

If I don't care for things I simply don't
look at them.

Every now and again along the way the self-seeker stops
to take stock:

SHE: I've over-educated myself in all the
things I shouldn't have known at all.

Mild Oats (1922)

★ ★ ★

My sense of my importance to the world
is relatively small. On the other hand, my
sense of my own importance to myself is
tremendous.

Present Indicative (1937)

Fame when it came was instant. And since it came with
The Vortex (1923), in which Coward played a young drug
addict, the popular image was ready made and the 'effete
young man' was happy to humour the Press:

I really have a frightfully depraved mind. I am never out of opium dens, cocaine dens and other evil places. My mind is a mass of corruption.

Commenting (ironically!) to the *Evening Standard* on the press speculation caused by the opening of the play:

No Press interviewer, photographer, or gossip-writer had to fight in order to see me, I was wide open to them all, smiling and burbling bright witticisms, giving my views on this and that, discussing such problems as whether or not the modern girl would make a good mother. I was photographed in every conceivable posi- tion... the legend of my modesty grew. I became extraordinarily unspoiled by my great success. As a matter of fact, I still am.
Present Indicative (1937)

Whatever the subject, an interviewer could be sure of a quotable answer. His idea of a perfect meal?

A little smoked salmon, a medium steak and perhaps some onions and chocolate ice cream. I've always been queer for chocolate!

On sleep:

I'm absolutely devoted to sleep. It is the most comforting, refreshing and pleasing thing anyone has vouchsafed for the human race.

Was there anything he could *not* do?

I could not dance in my own ballet.

The unqualified success of the early 1920s was, in many ways, both the best and the worst thing that happened to him. The eventual dilution of it certainly brought perspective.

GILDA: Success is far more perilous than failure, isn't it?

Design for Living (1932)

Though the fame would continue unabated, the acclaim would never reach the same decibel level as before, and for much of the rest of his life Coward would gently mock his own image:

In those days I was considered daring – now I'm practically Louisa M. Alcott.

(1970)

Asked by a lunch guest whether he had survived the war:

Like Mother Goddam, I shall always survive.

(1946)

He had very little patience with the would-be *enfants terribles* treading so rudely on his heels. In a 1932 song he could write that 'there's a younger Generation knock, knock, knocking at the door'. But now:

[*110*]

[I] cannot understand why the younger
generation, instead of knocking at the
door, should bash the fuck out of it.

Diaries (1957)

During the late fifties and early sixties he was the target
of much media browbeating – all of which he managed to
rise above:

It has been most gratifying… I now find
myself as big a celebrity as Debbie
Reynolds.

In this he was again recycling himself. In 1946 it had been
'Stalin and James Mason' – *Diaries* (1946).

The only thing that intrigues me is that
at the age of 56 I can still command such
general abuse.

Interview (1956)

★   ★   ★

My face is not my fortune but it must be
watched, if only for professional reasons.
It is now all right and the correct shape,
but it is no longer a young face and if it
were it would be macabre. It is strange
to examine it carefully and compare it
with early photographs.

Diaries (1956)

★   ★   ★

The battle, of course, will never end
until the grave closes over me and then,
oh dear, the balls that will be written
about me.
(1964)

★   ★   ★

I'm not particularly interested in being
remembered. It would be nice to have a
little niche in posterity but it's not one
of those dreadful things that haunts me.

★   ★   ★

Some day, I suspect, when Jesus has
definitely got me for a sunbeam, my
works may be adequately assessed.
Diaries (1956)

Through it all he kept faith with himself:

I'm an enormously talented man, and
there's no use pretending I'm not.
Sunday Express (1965)

★   ★   ★

The Almighty may write me out but I
shall not write myself out.
Today (3 October 1963)

Coward enjoyed the rewards success had brought him:

I have a Ritz mind and always have had.
It is a genuine hangover from when I was
really poor and had to endure bedbugs
and cheap digs and squalor. I am
unregenerate about this.

Diaries (1960)

★ ★ ★

The world has treated me very well – but then I haven't treated it so badly either.

On Ed Murrow's *Small World* (1959)

★ ★ ★

I've had a wonderful life. I've still got rhythm, I've got music, who could ask for anything more?

Diaries (1961)

When his reputation was re-established in the mid-1960s, in what he gleefully dubbed 'Dad's Renaissance', he accepted victory with the same insouciance as he had embraced defeat. On the *Dick Cavett Show* (1970) the normally imperturbable Cavett was clearly tongue-tied in the presence of the abnormally imperturbable Noël:

CAVETT: You're – you... what is the word when one has such terrific, prolific qualities?
NOËL: Talent.

★ ★ ★

People... have an insatiable passion for labelling everything with a motive. They search busily behind the simplest of my phrases, like old ladies peering under the bed for burglars, and are not content till they have unearthed some definite, and usually quite inaccurate, reason for my saying this or that.

★   ★   ★

My philosophy is as simple as ever – smoking, drinking, moderate sexual intercourse on a diminishing scale, reading and writing (not arithmetic). I have a selfish absorption in the well-being and achievement of Noël Coward.

Television interview (1970)

To what did he attribute his longevity?

To constant smoking and marrons glacés.

★   ★   ★

What – he was asked on his seventieth birthday – would he like as his epitaph?

He was much loved because he made people laugh and cry.

What were the two most beautiful things in the world?

Peace of mind and a sense of humour.

And how would he wish to be remembered?

By my charm.

His greatest single regret?

Not having taken more trouble with some of my work.

★　★　★

There will be lists of apocryphal jokes I never made and gleeful misquotations of words I never said. *What* a pity I shan't be here to enjoy them!

Diaries (1955)

★　★　★

With my usual watchful eye on posterity, I can only suggest to any wretched future biographer that he gets my daily engagement book and from that fills in anything he can find and good luck to him, poor bugger.

Diaries (December, 1969)